Elvis and the Junk

Written by Teresa Heapy

Illustrated by Martin and Ann Chatterton

Elvis was in a storm!
There were lots of things in the air.

There was a judder and a clang and some junk hit his rocket.
"Dear me! This is bad!" said Elvis.

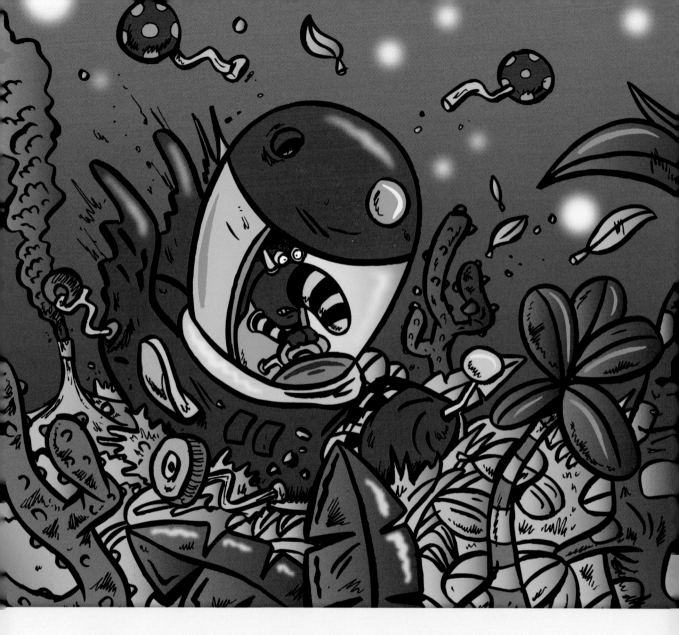

Elvis crash-landed on a planet.
"What is going on?" he said.

Elvis got out of his rocket and got a shock! There was a big red monster.

Elvis took the monster into his rocket.
"Come on! Do have a chair and some
sandwiches!" he said.

"Just the one, thank you," said
the monster.
"I like this. It is so good of you!"

"Look at my rocket!" said Elvis, and he started to weep. "It is such a mess!"

"I can mend it!" said the monster.
"I have a big stack of parts."

The monster mended the rocket.
"Wow! What a sight!" said Elvis.
"It looks so smart!"

"Just one little thing," said the monster.
"When will you come back?"

"When you ring me!" said Elvis.
"See you soon!"